The Apostles' Creed

illustrated for children
by Vicki Pastore

Paulist Press
New York/Mahwah, N.J.

For Kathy and Kathy, who love the Lord

Cover and interior design by Lynn Else

Library of Congress Cataloging-in-Publication Data

Pastore, Vicki.
    The Apostles' creed / illustrated for children by Vicki Pastore.
       p. cm.
    ISBN 978–0–8091–6738–8 (alk. paper)
    1. Apostles' Creed—Juvenile literature. I. Title.
    BT993.3.P37 2007
    238'.11—dc22

                                                    2006037689

Published by Paulist Press
997 Macarthur Boulevard
Mahwah, New Jersey 07430

www.paulistpress.com

Printed and bound in the
United States of America

I believe in God, the Father Almighty,

creator of heaven and earth.

I believe in Jesus Christ,
his only Son, Our Lord.

He was conceived by the
power of the
Holy Spirit and born
of the Virgin Mary.

He suffered under Pontius Pilate,

was crucified, died, and was buried.

He descended into hell.

On the third day he rose again.

He ascended
into heaven

and is seated at the right hand
of the Father.

He will come again to judge
the living and the dead.

I believe in the Holy Spirit,

the holy catholic church,

the communion of saints,

the forgiveness of sins,

the resurrection of the body,
and life everlasting.

The Apostles' Creed

I believe in God, the Father Almighty, creator
    of heaven and earth.
I believe in Jesus Christ, his only Son, Our Lord.
He was conceived by the power of the
    Holy Spirit and born of the Virgin Mary.
He suffered under Pontius Pilate, was
    crucified, died, and was buried.
He descended into hell.
On the third day he rose again.
He ascended into heaven and is seated
    at the right hand of the Father. He will
    come again to judge the living and the dead.
I believe in the Holy Spirit, the holy catholic church,
    the communion of saints, the forgiveness
    of sins, the resurrection of the body,
    and life everlasting.
Amen.